FIFTY WAYS TO PRACTISE BUSINESS ENGLISH

TIPS FOR ESL/EFL STUDENTS

KAREN RICHARDSON

WAYZGOOSE PRESS

CONTENTS

HOW TO USE THIS BOOK

It takes many hours to become proficient at anything — a sport, a hobby, a musical instrument, or a foreign language. Many thousands of hours, in fact! For a student of English, this can seem difficult to accomplish, and it's often hard to know where to start.

This book will help you learn and practise your business English, both at your workplace and while you are not working. If you are already taking English classes, some of the tips will help you get more out of your classes. If you're not taking English classes — and even if you are — other tips will give you ideas to try on your own. Not every idea will work for every language learner. That's why there are fifty. And a bonus tip! We feel sure that many of the ideas presented here will bring you results if you try them sincerely.

Here is a suggested method for using this book:

1. Read through all of the fifty-one tips without
   stopping.
2. Read through the tips again. Choose five or six that
   you think might work for you. Decide when you
   will try them, and for how long.
3. Choose different types of ideas: some for learning
   new business language, some for making the most
   of the digital opportunities all around us, some for
   improving your writing skills, some for practicing
   speaking. Choose some that you can practise with a
   friend, colleague, or language learning partner, and
   some that you can do alone. For your convenience,
   the tips are divided by category: *Digital Tools,
   Authentic Materials, Speaking, Listening, Business
   Writing, Workplace Language,* and *Business Skills.*
   However, the categories are general, and many
   activities fit into more than one area — similar to
   employees whose work is important to more than
   one department.
4. Each time you use one of the tips, make a note
   about how well it worked for you and why. Most of
   the tips will work best if you practise them several
   times (or even make them a habit). Don't try a tip
   only once and decide it's no good for you. Give the
   tips you try a few chances, at least.
5. Every few weeks, read through the tips again and
   choose some new ones. Stop using any methods
   that are not working for you, or think of ways that
   you can adapt them to make them more useful.

The most important advice, though, is to actually *do* the suggestions you read here. Wishing is not working. If you don't do the work, you won't see the results. Decide how you learn best. Don't make learning a chore. Count your successes, and see your failures as opportunities to improve.

Practise using English as often as you can. It doesn't have to be perfect; just do it. And do it as often and regularly as you can.

Finally, consider trying some of the other books in our *50 Ways to Practice* series. No one skill in English is really separate from the others. Speaking, listening, reading, writing, vocabulary, and grammar are all connected. Improving in one area will almost always bring improvements to other areas too.

Note: All of the links in this book worked at the time it was published (January 2023), and were accessible from North and South America, Europe, and many countries in Asia. If a particular link does not work for you, however, please send us an email at editor@wayzgoosepress.com, so we can update the book.

Spelling note: This book is written in British English, by its British author. There are a few differences between British English and American English spelling, such as *favourite/favorite*; *centre/center*; and *practise/practice*. In fact, you will notice that the other books in the *Fifty Ways to Practice* series are all in American English, because they had American authors—and so their titles are *Fifty Ways to*

Practice (Reading/Writing/Grammar/etc.), and this one is *Fifty Ways to Practise Business English*. Neither British nor American spelling is more "correct" than the other. When you do business in English around the world, you will meet many varieties of English. What version *you* should use depends on who you are working with. Be flexible!

PART 1

DIGITAL TOOLS

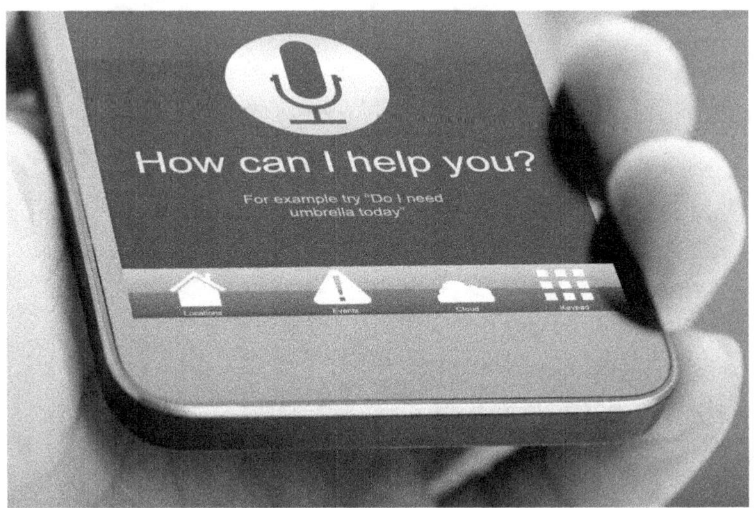

CHANGE THE LANGUAGE SETTINGS

Let's start with an easy one: social media. Change the language on your Facebook, Twitter, Instagram, and other social media accounts to English by going to your account settings. Choose the type of English : US English, British English, Australian, etc. Then do the same for your phone settings. Learn how to change the settings quickly so you can switch between your first language and English easily.

Update your profile on LinkedIn and make it bilingual – write everything in English next to the information in your first language. (If you don't already have a LinkedIn account, set one up at http://linkedin.com.)

Try using the voice dictation function on WhatsApp, Facebook Messenger, etc., in English, and see how well your device can understand your English pronunciation. You'll probably get some strange or funny results, so check your voice dictation messages carefully before you send them!

SIGN UP FOR BUSINESS ALERTS

Get alerts in English about a specific company or field of business. You can get the latest news sent to your email. Go to http://google.com/alerts, enter the name of the company or field of business you want to get news about (for example, *General Motors* or *solar energy*), choose how often you'd like to get the alerts, fill in any other information required, and make sure you choose English as the language you'd like to receive the alerts in.

There are of course other sources besides Google, that you can use to see what people are writing about your company or another company, such as one of these:

Talkwalker:
https://www.talkwalker.com/social-media-analytics-search

Awairo:
https://awario.com/social-media-monitoring-tools/

USE FREE ONLINE TRANSLATION TOOLS

Using online tools to help you translate your texts is not cheating. In fact, you'd almost be crazy *not* to use them for non-professional translation tasks. They can save you an enormous amount of time on your ordinary work tasks.

For example, if someone sends you a complicated message or email attachment in English, just copy and paste it into a translation tool such as DeepL:

https://www.deepl.com/en/translator

Although online translation tools don't always understand idioms and uncommon uses of certain words, they are usually good enough for you to understand the main content of the message.

However, remember to double-check any words or phrases that don't sound right to you. DeepL has an additional nice function that is linked to the Linguee online dictionary.

Click on any word in the text and the program will bring up the translations that it finds on Linguee. This will provide you with alternative words and synonyms and give you a choice of translations.

4

TRANSLATE WITH YOUR PHONE CAMERA

Some of the newer translation tools, such as the one from DeepL, have apps that use your phone camera. Just open the app, point the camera at a text, choose your languages, and almost by magic, the text will appear like the camera reads it, and underneath with the translated version. You don't even need to type anything in. Try it on a restaurant menu or a company brochure.

If you often need to translate from one specific language to another, you can choose this in as your default setting; e.g., Spanish to English. Just point the camera at the text you want to translate, take a photo, and the text will appear in your target language. Other translation tools and apps are also available, such as Google Translate, Microsoft Translator, iTranslate, Dialog, and many more.

KEEP TRACK OF THE WEATHER

Many people, and British people in particular, like to talk about the weather. If you have a business partner in a different country who you often talk to, or a company that you often have meetings with, add the city where they work to your weather app. Make sure the language setting is English, and look at the weather forecast before you talk to your business partners. Integrate the words that you read on the app into your small talk to help build a better, friendlier business relationship.

For example, if your partner is in Manchester, England, add this city to your app. Then, use the words that you read on the app, such as *drizzle, gusty,* and *rainfall* when you next talk to your business partner; for example, *I see you've had quite a lot of rainfall there in the last few days. What's it like now? Is it still drizzling?*

USE TO-DO LISTS

Download an app that helps you manage your to-do lists, and write everything into it in English. Include action verbs, such as

- *prepare the budget presentation*
- *get hold of Mr X*
- *proofread the report*

and so on. Add deadlines to your entries, such as

- *Send conference proposal <u>by the end of the month</u>.*

Write entries into your paper desk appointment diary in English, too.

PART 2

AUTHENTIC MATERIAL

READ BREAKING BUSINESS NEWS

Download apps that provide you with real-time updates and breaking news in the business field you're interested in. For example, if you're interested in financial news and up-to-date market news, download an app like the Bloomberg's Business News app, the CNBC Stock Market & Business App, or TheStreet App. Business Insider lets you choose the topics you're interested in and save articles to read later, as does the Financial Times app.

Some of the apps have articles you can listen to as well. Do this either with your eyes closed so you can concentrate more on what you hear, or read the article at the same time as you listen to it to increase your understanding and to listen to different accents. Al Jazeera's English app offers live TV and video-on-demand that you can filter for business content.

When you have chosen and downloaded your favourite business news app, allow it to send you push notifications for breaking news, so you won't be able to guess or control when the next information will appear on your screen. The more random it is, the more likely it is to stay in your memory.

LEARN A BUSINESS WORD OF THE DAY

Download a 'business word of the day' app or sign up for a daily business word of the day email. Make a habit of reading and listening to the pronunciation of the new word every single day; maybe at breakfast or during your commute to work. Write your own work-related sentences and then try to use that word in a sentence during the day.

If you have difficulty thinking of your own sentence, put the word or phrase into the search field on a sentence website such as Sentence Stack https://sentencestack.com/ or Sentence Dictionary, https://sentencedict.com/, read the sentences they offer (usually sourced from the web), choose a business-related one you like, and make that your example sentence.

Good business word of the day apps include the Merriam-Webster Word of the Day and the New York Times Word of the Day. If German is your first language, try the Business Spotlight Word of the Day app.

GET THE MOST OUT OF VIDEOS

Watch videos online that are related to your field of business. Put on the automated subtitles if the speaker isn't easy to understand. The subtitles may not be perfect, but they are usually not bad and can be quite helpful.

Try to think outside the box a little bit. Don't only watch company-made videos; also try searching for training videos, such as 'How to drive / operate a forklift', 'How to make a hospital bed', or 'How to make a perfect coffee'.

In fact, watch anything that even vaguely interests you. You'll not only hear useful language, but you might learn a new skill, too. Unboxing videos are also very interesting, especially if the person is unboxing one of your company's products or that of a rival company. You'll find a large number of unboxing videos for electronic devices.

Watch 'tips and tricks' videos for the same devices for some good insights about what customers think of certain products and even what features they feel are missing.

WATCH TED BUSINESS TALKS

Even though they've been around for a while, don't forget TED talks. TED stands for technology, entertainment, and design. The website http://www.ted.com has an extremely large sub-section called 'TED business', which at the time this book was written contains around 4,000 talks in audio or video format – often with the script so that you can read along while listening.

TED also has ready-made playlists so you don't have to choose what to listen to next. The playlists are made by well-known business people or authors such as Dan Pink, or are grouped into categories such as '12 talks on diversity in the workplace', '6 talks to save you time at work', or '7 talks to boost your team's productivity'.

You can also find many TED talks on YouTube.

GO TO YOUR COMPANY WEBSITE

Read the English version of your company's website carefully. How understandable is it? How convincing is it? How interesting is it for potential new customers or clients? Play devil's advocate (that is, take the opposite point of view). Think of reasons someone should *not* buy your products or *not* use your services. Make a list of questions in English such as:

- *Do I really need this?*
- *Why don't I just go somewhere else that offers something similar for a cheaper price?*
- *Is this really better than what the competitors are offering?*

Try to answer these questions using just the information available on the website. If you can't show that your company's products or services are the best available according to the website, decide how to fix this. Make some suggestions for improvements.

If there isn't an English version of your company's website, start translating it. Then hire a professional translator and compare your translation to theirs.

WATCH DIFFERENT VERSIONS OF
BUSINESS-RELATED TV SHOWS

Find an easy-to-understand, popular business-related TV series whose original version is English, but that has been dubbed into your language. A few examples: *The Office* (there is a British version and an American version of this series), *Superstore, Mad Men, Suits, Better Call Saul, Silicon Valley,* and *Start Up.*

Watch an episode in your language and then watch the same episode again in English. How much more do you understand now that you know what is going to happen?

If it's still difficult to understand, put on the subtitles in English so that you can read along with what you hear on screen. You can do the same with films, but the nice thing about a series is that the episodes are shorter, and the story line will be fresher in your mind when you watch in English.

If you are really short of time, watch trailers for films or shows on streaming services – first in your language, and then again in English. How do they compare? Which language version of the trailer most makes you want to watch the whole film or series?

ADD TO YOUR BUSINESS CARDS AND EMAIL SIGNATURES

Translate your own business card. Do the same for those of your colleagues.

Write the translations on the back of the cards, and use them as vocabulary cards or flashcards to check whether you remember the translations.

Add further details (if you can find space) such as when the company was founded, where its HQ (headquarters) is, and who the owners or board members are.

Then translate your email signature. If it is appropriate, add it permanently to your outgoing emails. Notice other people's English email signatures when you receive them.

READ, READ, READ

Subscribe to a specialist magazine in English – or to the English version of a company's newsletter.

Read your suppliers' and competitors' websites in English.

Read the English section of an instruction manual, or the warranty of any electronic item.

In fact, simply read and try to understand anything business-related that you can get your hands on. The more you do this, the easier it will become.

DESCRIBE PROCESSES AND GIVE CLEAR INSTRUCTIONS

Go to the library. Read business and specialist magazines in English and borrow a factual (non-fiction) book in English. Anything that describes a process can be useful to read. It doesn't have to be business-related – it could be a cookbook or a magazine about how to grow vegetables or build furniture. (If your library does not have English materials, you can search online.)

Notice how the language of the instructions is structured: *First, second, then, next, after a while, finally,* etc. Write these structure words into your vocabulary notebook and use them to describe a work process that you are familiar with.

PART 3

SPEAKING

PRACTISE WITH AN ENGLISH-SPEAKING PARTNER

Find someone you can talk to at least twice a week for about thirty minutes. This could be a language teacher or trainer, of course, but it could also be a (fluent) speaker of the language you'd like to learn.

For example, your partner is English-speaking, and you are Spanish-speaking – you both want to practise the other's language. Can you make yourself understood? Do you understand them?

Practise comprehension rather than grammar and vocabulary – look that up later. Even a non-teacher will be able to tell you if they understand you or not.

SET UP A REGULAR ENGLISH LUNCH OR COFFEE BREAK

If your colleagues would also like to practise their English, meet for an English-speaking lunch or coffee break once a week. You probably won't all have exactly the same level of English or the same knowledge of vocabulary and grammar, so you'll be able to help each other. And if none of you knows the word you are searching for, then allow yourself to 'cheat' and look it up. That way you'll all learn something.

If there isn't a work colleague who wants to join you for a regular English chat, perhaps there's someone who takes the same commuter train or bus, someone you could walk to work with, or even another dog-walker, Nordic-walker, or hill climber (depending on what you do in your private life). There's no reason not to think outside the box (or work canteen) a little bit.

TALK TO YOURSELF

If you can't find someone to talk to regularly in English – or even if you can – talk to yourself in English, too. Go out for a walk through a large park or in the woods – go any place where no one will look at you strangely when you talk aloud to yourself.

Use the time to practise the speech or presentation you need to give, a conversation you'll soon have with a customer, a sales pitch, different ways of introducing yourself, etc. The list of things you can talk to yourself about is endless.

Physical movement is known to improve our ability to learn. Speaking words out loud and not just going over them silently in your head will increase your confidence, and show you where you need to look up missing words or check pronunciation. At the very least, you'll always have an attentive audience!

MAKE A VIDEO WALKTHROUGH OF YOUR COMPANY

Make a virtual walkthrough of your company or workplace.

Start by introducing yourself and your company, then walk around while filming. Either describe everything you see as you see it, or film in silence and add a voice-over description afterwards.

If your colleagues are happy to help you, when you get to them, ask them who they are and what they do, and have them introduce themselves on your video.

SCRIPT AND FILM A "WHY MY COMPANY IS THE BEST" VIDEO

Have you ever seen an advert where the owner of a company describes their company and what it does, and says why it's the best company in the world (or at least in its field)?

Write a script, practice it a few times, and then film an advert in which you enthusiastically tell your viewers all the good things about your company and why you like to work there.

MAKE A "WELCOME TO OUR COMPANY" VIDEO FOR VISITORS FROM FAR AWAY

Make a recording (video or voice) welcoming foreign visitors to your company.

The recording should give them useful information that will help them get around your building. Explain, for example, where they can park, when the canteen is open and how it works, which elevators and doors to use to reach certain people and sections, which departments are on each floor, etc.

Watch or listen to your recording, identify sections that you are not happy with, or words and phrases you could say better, and do a 'take two'.

Continue with further 'takes' (versions) until you are completely satisfied with your recording.

22

TALK AROUND THE TOPIC

If you can't think of a word you need – one that is important to what you want to say – try talking *around* it. Practise strategies to describe the word you can't remember or don't know, as well as phrases to 'buy you time' to think further or ask for help. The person you are speaking to will probably understand what you want to say. Learn these phrases and integrate them into your spoken English:

To describe a word or idea:

- *I'm sure you know what I mean, it's similar to….*
- *You use it to ….*
- *The thing we need to….*
- *It looks like a …*
- *It's what happens when you…*

Phrases to buy yourself some time:

- *Oh, what's it called again, the thing that… ?*
- *The word is on the tip of my tongue.*
- *Oh, what is the word I'm looking for?*

If you do this in a natural-sounding way, the other person will probably say or suggest the word you are looking for. This strategy is no different to what native speakers do when they can't remember a word, so you will sound completely fluent.

USE FILLERS

Another way to sound more fluent is to use 'fillers' when you speak. Little words and phrases such as *Well, Ermm, Um, You know, So, By the way, Yeah* and *umm, like* … can be incredibly useful.

Listen to native and fluent speakers, such as your business partners, or watch business talks on YouTube, TedTalks, etc. Make a note of all the small filler words they use.

In fact, the people you are talking with will most likely appreciate this, because every time you use a filler, it gives them time to think about what you have already said and what they want to say next.

For the same reason, a short pause is never a bad thing. A pause gives everybody essential time to process what has been said and to consider what the next words should be.

PART 4

LISTENING

LISTEN ON THE MOVE

Research shows that movement not only helps you learn, but helps you remember information, too. Listen to business news podcasts instead of music while you are doing your morning exercises, commuting, or taking a walk.

Try to understand the main idea of the story or report that you are listening to and make a mental (or physical) note of the timing of sections you had difficulty understanding (for example, *at 17 minutes into the audio*), and listen again to these sections when you are back home.

SUBSCRIBE TO BUSINESS NEWS PODCASTS

Subscribe to business news podcasts from around the world. Listen to different accents and other kinds of English, not only in (standard) British English or American English. Even within British English, you will find many different speaker accents – Scottish or Northern Irish, for example.

Search for audio reports and podcasts by people with the same or similar accent to the people you often do business with, so that you can get used to that accent.

For example, if you have business partners in India, listen to podcasts that interest you and are relevant to your work on Forbes India, which has a variety of podcasts on different business subjects, or listen to 'The Week on Dalal Street' on Money Control:

https://www.moneycontrol.com/news/shows/the-week-on-dalal-street/

which offers a weekly summary of financial news.

Just search for business podcasts plus the name of the country or region you are interested in (for example, 'business podcasts South Africa').

Don't limit yourself to native speakers, either. There are plenty of business podcasts in English from countries whose first language is not English, but who use English for international business communication.

LISTEN TO AMERICAN ENGLISH AND BRITISH ENGLISH AUDIO AND VIDEO

If you want to listen to native speakers, search for business news websites that provide free audio in the form of discussions or news from both sides of the Atlantic.

For example, the *Economist* has a daily podcast called 'The Intelligence' that comes from London and New York, so you can listen to both American and British accents and even compare the way the speakers say the same words.

The *Financial Times* has a large range of podcasts in British English, which are also kept in their archives. Start by listening to short ones or ones that really interest you, and then challenge yourself with longer ones.

NPR (*National Public Radio*) has a daily podcast in American English about 10 minutes long that discusses the three biggest stories that day.

CNBC's 'Make It' has a lot of short business-related videos especially interesting for younger businesspeople such as

'Side Hustles', 'Startups', and 'Young Success'. The videos are mostly in American English. You can usually read the script of the video on the website at the same time as you watch the video in a corner of the screen.

LISTEN TO BUSINESS-RELATED AUDIOBOOKS

Listen to audiobooks whose topic is business or fiction that takes place in a business setting. Best of all are those that involve your field of work and use business language you already know a little or are familiar with but not completely confident using.

While you listen, make a note about any business terminology that is used repeatedly. For example, if you work in the legal profession, you could try books by John Grisham for legal terms. If you work in the hotel or catering business, or in finance, there are plenty of books you could try.

Obviously, listening to a book in English is not the same as listening to one in your first language, so why not slow it down slightly? Most devices allow audiobooks to be played at a reduced speed. See how much you can reduce the speed and not lose quality. Maybe try listening to it at '0.7x or 0.8x of the normal 'narration speed' or 'playback speed'.

Another tip is to listen to books that you have already read, and read books that you have already listened to.

If a book in its original version is too challenging, try business English-related 'graded readers', which have been adapted to make them easier for learners. There are many business titles available such as 'Collins ELT Readers -- Amazing Entrepreneurs & Business People (Level 4)' or 'Sprint' from https://www.penguinreaders.co.uk/ladybird-books/sprint/ at Level B1+.

PRACTISE YOUR LISTENING SKILLS

Become a better listener to improve your English. Practise how to say short phrases that show you are listening when the speaker pauses, such as *Really? Unbelievable! That's interesting.*

Another method is to interrupt the speaker with your comments. This will both slow them down, allowing you to process what they've already said, and encourage them to provide more information, both of which will hopefully help your understanding. It will also show the speaker that you are really listening and paying attention.

One simple and polite way of doing this is to repeat back the last thing that someone said and turn it into a question:

Speaker: ...and then they cancelled the order! So...
You: They cancelled the order?
Speaker: Yes, that's right, they did. So we had to...

PART 5

BUSINESS WRITING

WRITE USEFUL BUSINESS TIPS FOR VISITORS

Imagine that you need to visit a subsidiary on the other side of the world. Think about what cultural and etiquette information you would like to know before you go. Make a list of your questions.

Then think about what information about business culture and etiquette would be useful for foreign visitors to *your* country / place of work (for example, for work exchange students / interns on international placements).

Write a document titled 'Tips for Visitors'. Save it, and keep going back to it to improve and update it. You could even send this to future visitors when it's finished.

LET WORD DO THE WORK

One of the best and easiest ways of checking your English spelling and grammar is simply to write a draft of whatever it is you need to write – an email, a report, a memo, etc. – into a Word document. Make sure you have the language set to the type of English you want to practise; e.g. English (UK) or English (US). Word will then automatically underline any spelling or grammar mistakes it thinks you made and give you suggestions to correct these.

You can trust the spelling checker (although it won't catch everything), and you can use the grammar checker to double-check sections you think might be incorrect, but do not assume that Word's automatic corrections are correct 100% of the time. For example, here is a "mistake" Word found when checking this book:

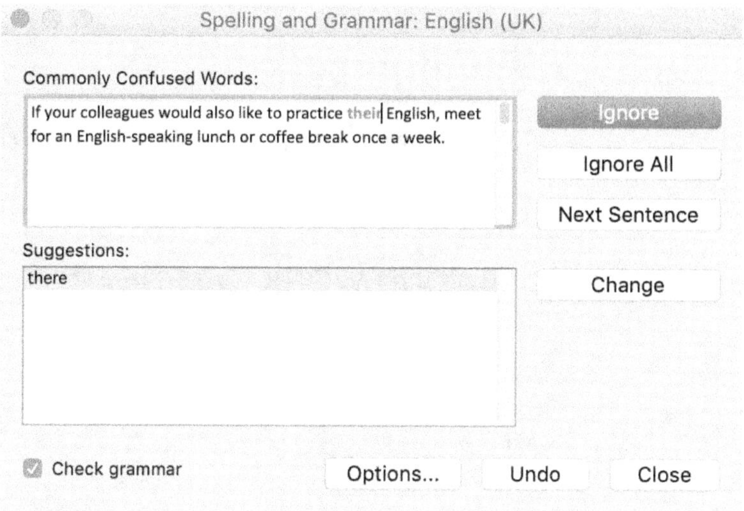

In this sentence, the original *their* is correct.

However, it's good to know that Word thinks you should check your grammar before you send or print your document. *There, they're,* and *their* are commonly confused words, and it doesn't hurt to double-check them.

Make sure you remember the corrections for next time! Your aim is to have fewer and fewer words underlined with each new document you write.

SUMMARISE YOUR WORK CALENDAR

Read today's appointment diary entries. Go through your last two weeks' diary or appointment calendar entries, and read the next two weeks' notes, too.

Talk to yourself (or a willing listener) and explain what work tasks you <u>did</u> in the past two weeks and what you <u>are going to do</u> in the coming two weeks. Don't forget to talk about what you <u>are doing</u>, or <u>have already done</u>, today. Pay careful attention to the tenses you use.

After you have talked through the four-week period, write a summary of the month's tasks and achievements.

WRITE A MAGAZINE PROFILE

You're going to be interviewed for a business magazine profile! Make notes about how you would like to be described. What words would you like people to use when they talk about you as a businessperson?

If you like, read some magazine profiles of other businesspeople for inspiration and ideas. You can make your profile completely true, or use your imagination to all about "future you"!

Variation: Imagine you have just joined the company, and no one knows anything about you or your previous work. Write a short piece about yourself for the company website.

IDENTIFY THE KEY SKILLS FOR YOUR JOB

Write an advertisement for own job. Think about the key skills someone doing your job should have: for example, they should be able to work well under time pressure, they should be able to use XXX software, they should work well in teams, etc. You can check your contract for a list of your official duties, but there are other "soft" personal skills for your work that you understand best.

When you have a list of skills, then turn each one around in a sentence, like these:

- *I am able to work well under time pressure.*
- *I can use XXX software.*
- *I work well in teams.*

If these skills are not already listed on your CV, update your English CV now.

APPLY FOR YOUR DREAM JOB

Think about a job you would have liked, but that you never did – your dream job in another life, perhaps. A ship's captain, an elephant trainer, a fighter pilot, a mountain guide, a wine taster… anything!

Write a covering letter stating why you would be the best person for this job and what you can bring to the position. Create imaginary skills and qualifications to improve your chances of getting an interview for the position.

WRITE TO YOURSELF

Write an email to yourself in English, reminding yourself what you need to do, what you should get done, and what you want to achieve next week. Include dates, times, topics, and places as well as names and positions of people you will be talking to.

Some people do this at the start of every work week as a way of creating a to-do list.

You will also find that just writing information down and reading it again will help you remember it naturally.

PART 6

WORKPLACE LANGUAGE

USE THE LANGUAGE OF INTERESTS AND HOBBIES FOR BUSINESS PURPOSES

Do you love cycling, gardening, or playing football? Do you read specialist magazines, websites, or blogs? Do you watch videos, contribute to forums, or correspond with other people about your interests?

It's very likely that the language you use to talk about your passions could be used in a business context.

For example, think about the preparations you need to make for a cycling trip and the verbs you might use: *make sure, double-check, plan, expect, pack, carry,* etc. These can be equally useful to talk about a business trip.

Can you explain how and when to plant vegetables and what happens next? You can certainly use the same words to describe a business process: *First, make…, Next,… Then,… If all goes well,… After a few months,… ,* etc.

And how did that football match go? Why did you lose? What could you have done differently? How will you make sure the results are better next time? All the phrases to review what went wrong and how to get better results are transferable to business English: *We should have…, Unfortunately, we…, We didn't expect…, Next time, we'll…,* etc.

TRY YOUR NATIVE LANGUAGE

If you can't remember that important word or don't know how to pronounce it, another strategy is to simply say the word in your native language (or another language you know).

So many of the words we use in business English have common roots, or are even **cognates** (words that are the same or almost the same in two different languages), so it's at least worth a try.

This won't always work, but, especially in the world of global business English, it will probably work more often that you think!

Example: You want to say that you need to send an engineer and a mechanic to a subsidiary, but you are unsure how to say those three essential words: *engineer, mechanic,* and *subsidiary.*

Here you can see that if you try the words in another language, your listeners will at least be able to understand two out of three, which is not a bad start.

English	Spanish	French	German
engineer	ingeniero	ingénieur	Ingenieur
mechanic	mecánico	mécanicien	Mechaniker
subsidiary	filial	filiale	Tochtergesellschaft

ANNOTATE A PHOTO OF YOUR WORKPLACE

Take a photo of your desk, your workbench, your office, etc. Print it out and write the names of all the items you see on the photo. As well as all the obvious items such as a desk and lamp, go into detail and write the names of items you might not always notice at first, such as paperclips, a coaster for your coffee mug, a tin of cough sweets, etc. Look up any words you don't know.

Use the photo as a kind of visual vocabulary card. Say the words out loud as you touch the items. Then turn the photo over, look at the area you took a photo of, and try to remember the names of all the items.

Do this for other workplace areas such as a conference room, the reception area, the kitchen, and even outside areas such as the parking lot or entrance gate to increase your business and company-specific vocabulary.

COLLECT USEFUL STANDARD PHRASES

Standard phrases are called *standard* for a reason: everyone understands them, and possibly even expects to read them in an email or letter. Once you have learnt and remembered a few useful ones, you can use them again and again.

Write a list of standard phrases you could use:

- on the phone
- in an email
- when welcoming or introducing someone
- starting or ending a meeting
- joining and leaving a meeting in person or online
- in the type of business document you often have to write (a report, an order, a discount or payment request, a payment reminder, an apology, etc.)

Make folders on your desktop for different types of tasks, or write them out and place them next to your phone, so you can easily access the standard phrases you need to use regularly. However, type these out rather than copying and pasting, as the act of typing the words (or even writing them by hand) will fix them better in your memory.

COLLECT EMAIL HELLOS AND GOODBYES

Check all your emails for salutations (greetings such as *Dear Mr Kim*) and sign-offs (such as *Best regards,*). Copy them into a document or spreadsheet.

Which are used most frequently? Do you notice that salutations or sign-offs change after people exchange several emails? Can you notice a difference in which ones are used more often by native speakers / men / women / younger or older colleagues? Which ones sound more formal / informal / friendly / distant?

Think about which language would be most appropriate for your next emails with your colleagues and business contacts.

USE STANDARD BUSINESS EMAIL PHRASES

Go through your English emails (and ones you can get from colleagues, if they are not private). Check for standard phrases that businesspeople use in their emails. Check and compare the style (formal / informal / neutral).

Are there any friendly opening questions or last comments, such as *I hope you are well* or *Did you have a good weekend?* Try adding one or two of these to your next email exchanges and notice whether you get some back in response.

Note that often this type of language is cultural. If you receive emails from people from different countries, see if you notice any patterns. You don't have to exactly match the style of the person you are emailing, but if you come close, it can make the relationship seem warmer.

COLLECT WORDS AND PHRASES

Create your own vocabulary book in a stylish paper notebook that you will want to keep nearby.

Make a note of all the important words that you had to look up when you were reading business documents, texts, and articles. Write both the word and the sentence that it appeared in so that you have the context. Add other forms of the word; for example, if the word was *interview*, write other forms such as *interviewer* and *interviewee*, and add the verbs that are used with it such as *hold an interview, attend an interview, invite someone to an interview,* etc. When you read or hear the word in other places, write that sentence into your notebook, too. The more examples you can add, the more you'll feel confident using the word.

Vocabulary in the world of work changes often, and there are special terms and phrases for different industries and jobs. No standard English textbook will have all of the vocabulary you need for *your* job. But you can create your own!

If you don't want to write in a notebook, create a file or list on your phone or computer. The great thing about an electronic document is that after you have written a few entries, you can alphabetise the key words so they are easy to find as your document gets longer. Sort the words into categories or colour-code them.

Anything you do with the list and your notebook so that you actively use it will help you remember and improve your vocabulary.

RECORD AND KEEP BUSINESS LANGUAGE WHILE YOU ARE OUT

Keep a notebook or use the 'notes' function on your phone to collect English business language you come across while you are out and about. Make notes of the language used on billboard ads, on the sides and backs of company vehicles, on other signs that are written in English or in more than one language – for example, those at the train station.

If you don't have your notebook with you, take photos and write the language into your book or electronic lists later, if that's more convenient.

Imagine that you need to call the company on the billboard, van, etc., to enquire about their services or products. Use some of the words and phrases that you wrote down when you create your questions.

RETELL AN ARTICLE USING KEY WORDS

Find a 1-3 page paper or online business article that interests you. Tear it out of the magazine or print it off the website. On each page, highlight 8-10 key words or phrases to help you retell the article. Write just these words on another piece of paper or in a document to make a 'cheat sheet'.

Use this to retell the article (to yourself, to someone else, or record yourself speaking). Next, write a short summary of the article. Finally, compare your summary and retelling to the original article. Did you miss any key facts or points? If so, why? Did you choose the wrong key words? Did you not highlight enough words in the phrase?

Consider what you can do to improve your performance, and then repeat the task with a different article. Each time you do this task, you'll get better at deciding which words and phrases to highlight, and consequently you'll get better at retelling the article.

PART 7

BUSINESS SKILLS

SIGN UP FOR CONTINUING PROFESSIONAL DEVELOPMENT COURSES

Sign up for a CPD course in English. If you have the time and money available to travel – or you can convince your boss to send you – sign up for a course that takes place somewhere that English is spoken as the first language or official language of administration.

Alternatively, attend a course nearby where the instruction is in English – possibly because the trainer's first language is English, or because the course is open to people from around the world and so is taught in English. If possible, attend the course in person. That way you will also have the opportunity to practise and improve your small talk skills during the breaks and at any evening get-togethers.

If you are responsible for paying for your own CPD, you might be able to combine it with a holiday. How does a CPD course on the island of Malta or Bermuda, or on the wild coasts of Scotland or Ireland sound to you?

SIGN UP FOR A BUSINESS MOOC

Try a MOOC (massive open online course) run by a business college or reputed university. Go to

http://www.mooc-list.com/

or another platform such as

http://www.coursera.org or

https://www.mooc.org/

and find a course that you're interested in. Many are free to attend, and run from a few weeks to a few months, although you can usually do them at your own pace.

During the course, you'll be required to watch videos, do some reading, answer questions, contribute to forums (perhaps), and take tests.

If you want a certificate at the end of the course to add to your CV / resume or LinkedIn profile, you can usually get one for a small fee.

SPONSORS, SPONSORSHIP, AND SPONSORING

Who sponsors your local or favourite sports team? How visible is the name of the company – is it on the team clothing? Where else can you read the name of the sponsor? Is the name on the pitch or the stadium? In the programmes? Why does this company sponsor this team? It is a good fit? What do each of the parties get out of the sponsorship?

Think about which team or group you would like to sponsor and why.

Prepare an elevator pitch / mini presentation for the team manager or owner, saying why your company should be their next sponsors.

SUMMARISE AND RETELL BUSINESS NEWS

Read a long (at least two pages, but preferably more) article or report about a business topic, such as a merger or takeover or the launch of a new product or service.

Decide how you would summarise it so you could explain the main points to a friend or colleague. Then record yourself giving the summary.

Send the recording to yourself as an email attachment and open it a week later. Listen to the recording and decide how well you did.

CREATE AN ENGLISH VERSION OF YOUR PRESENTATION

Are you creating slides for a presentation? Once you are happy with the slides in your first language, create a second set in English.

This is a great opportunity to practise writing concisely and clearly, and to check that you know important vocabulary in English for your job.

And you never know – perhaps one day you'll be asked to give a similar presentation to an international audience, and then you'll already have your slides prepared.

COLLECT ADVERTS, BROCHURES, AND FLYERS

Collect company adverts, brochures, and flyers in English. Identify useful language so that you can explain these companies to someone else. Think about what vocabulary in these materials you can also use to describe your own company and your own work.

Does the printed material provide clear information about the field of business, the services and products, the owners, the company history, its headquarters, etc.? If not, look up this information and write it onto the printed material.

BONUS TIP!
LEARN WITH EASY-TO-UNDERSTAND LANGUAGE VIDEOS

Watch the videos *12 useful phrasal verbs for Business English* and *English for Online Meetings - Clear Communication* created by British business English teacher Vicki Hollett and her American partner Jay Silber.

These are just two of many, many useful language learning videos on their award-winning YouTube channel *Simple English Videos:*

https://www.youtube.com/watch?v=FOKZInuPqTw

The videos on the channel vary in length, from around 3 to 12 minutes long, and they are light-hearted and easy to understand. They deal with a huge variety of topics such as difficult pronunciations, common mistakes, American vs. British English, tricky grammar points, easily confused words, and fun quizzes to test your English.

AFTERWORD

Learning another language is never fast, but the *Fifty Ways to Practice* series will speed things up by showing you how to practice (or practise!) more efficiently and effectively, both inside and outside the classroom. It is useful for beginning through advanced levels. The *Fifty Ways to Practice* series offers short, practical guides to different areas of English language study for motivated students.

Note: We have priced these *Fifty Ways to Practice* guides very inexpensively, because we want education and learning to be available to as many people as possible. However, our authors are highly qualified professionals who work hard to create these books. If these books are useful to you, please recommend them to your friends—but please do not share them freely. Our authors will continue to write excellent and cheap books for you if they make a little money. That way, we all win. Thank you for your support!

If you have comments or suggestions (such as ideas for future books that you would find useful), feel free to contact the publisher at editor@wayzgoosepress.com, check out the offerings on our publishing website at http://wayzgoosepress.com, or join us on Facebook.

To be notified about the release of new 50 Ways titles, as well as other new titles and special contests, events, and sales from Wayzgoose Press, please sign up for our mailing list through the website or this link: http://eepurl.com/bSGudb (We send email infrequently, and you can unsubscribe at any time.)